PRESENTED TO

ON THE OCCASION OF

FROM

DATE

A LITTLE INSPIRATION

FOR A *Prayer* FILLED DAY

BARBOUR
PUBLISHING

© 2003 by Barbour Publishing, Inc.

ISBN 1-59310-231-3

Compiled by Richard A. Hasler.

Published by Barbour Publishing, Inc., P.O. Box 719, Uhrichsville, Ohio 44683, www.barbourbooks.com

*Our mission is to publish and distribute inspirational products offering exceptional value
and biblical encouragement to the masses.*

Printed in China.
5 4 3 2 1

Adoration sets the tone for the entire prayer.
It reminds us Whom we are addressing,
Whose presence we have entered,
Whose attention we have gained.

BILL HYBELS

Too Busy Not to Pray

All great prayer, all liberating worship,
all lasting encounters with God,
begin with praise and rejoicing.

LLOYD OGILVIE

Let God Love You

Yank some of the groans out of your prayers,
and shove in some shouts.

BILLY SUNDAY

The sooner I forget myself in the desire
that He may be glorified,
the richer will the blessing be
that prayer will bring to myself.

ANDREW MURRAY

With Christ in the School of Prayer

Are you so identified with the Lord's life
that you are simply a child of God,
continually talking to Him and
realizing all things come from His hands?

OSWALD CHAMBERS

My Utmost for His Highest

The spirit of prayer makes us
so intimate with God that we
scarcely pass through an experience
before we speak to Him about it.

O. HALLESBY
Prayer

If you are God's child,
there is this expectant line of communication
always between you and God.
Your experience may be a dreary wilderness,
a sea of despair, a dusty, sandy waste with no shade—
but over all is a line of communication
between you and God.

OSWALD CHAMBERS
The Place of Help

Mental prayer is nothing else. . .
but being on terms of friendship with God,
frequently conversing in secret with Him.

TERESA OF AVILA

Life of St. Teresa

Prayer abases intellect and pride,
crucifies vainglory,
and signs our spiritual bankruptcy,
and all these are hard for flesh and blood to bear.

E. M. BOUNDS

Power through Prayer

The worst sin is prayerlessness.

P. T. FORSYTH

The Soul of Prayer

If your prayers are not being answered,
search your heart,
and see if there is someone you have yet to forgive.

LEHMAN STRAUSS

Sense and Nonsense about Prayer

Prayer is literally
talking things over in confidence—
in full confidence with God.
Sometimes the substitution of
the word "confidence" for
the word "faith" helps.

Eugenia Price

Leave Yourself Alone

Prayers are heard in heaven
very much in proportion to our faith.
Little faith will get very great mercies,
but great faith still greater.

CHARLES H. SPURGEON

Gleanings Among the Sheaves: Believing Prayer

The man is perfect in faith who can
come to God in the utter dearth of
his feelings and desires,
without a glow or an inspiration,
with the weight of low thoughts, failures, neglects,
and wandering forgetfulness,
and say to Him, "Thou art my refuge."

George MacDonald

Unspoken Sermons

During the course of the day,
I frequently ask the Lord to give me wisdom
to use the knowledge that I have and
to give me perspective and understanding,
particularly when difficult situations arise.

BEN CARSON

Think Big

I have often wished that
I was a more decent man. . . .
Nevertheless, amid the
greatest difficulties of my administration,
when I could not see any other resort,
I would place my whole reliance upon God.

ABRAHAM LINCOLN

Letter to Baltimore Presbyterian Synod

I can worry myself into a state of
spiritual ennui over questions like
"What good does it do to pray
if God already knows everything?"
Jesus silences such questions.
He prayed; so should we.

PHILIP YANCEY

The Jesus I Never Knew

All healing is looked upon by
the Bible as a victory of God. . . .
He accepts all our prayers
for the healing of the sick.

PAUL TOURNIER

The Adventure of Living

God cares about every area of our lives,
and God wants us to ask for help.

BEN CARSON

Think Big

Worry about nothing;
pray about everything.

CHARLES SWINDOLL

Laugh Again

Prayer is the coming into awareness,
the practicing of attention,
the nurturing and development of
personal intensity before God.

Eugene Peterson

Reversed Thunder:
The Revelation of John and the Praying Imagination

True prayer is not to be found in
the words of the mouth
but in the thoughts of the heart.

GREGORY THE GREAT

Commentary on the Book of Job

We always have God's full attention.

Our part is to give Him ours.

EUGENIA PRICE

Leave Yourself Alone

As the saying goes:
He who thinks of many things
thinks of nothing and accomplishes no good.
How much more must prayer possess the heart
exclusively and completely if it is to be a good prayer.

MARTIN LUTHER

A Simple Way to Pray, for a Good Friend

Too many of our prayers—
private and public—
are just browsing amongst possible petitions,
not down to cases at all.
We expect nothing from our prayers
except perhaps a euphoric feeling.

CATHERINE MARSHALL
Adventures in Prayer

If we are not entirely dedicated
to our own prayers,
we should not expect God
to waste time with us.

CHARLES L. ALLEN
Prayer Changes Things

There is nothing that makes us love a man
so much as praying for him. . . .
By considering yourself as an advocate with
God for your neighbors and acquaintances,
you would never find it hard to be
at peace with them yourself.

WILLIAM LAW
A Serious Call

The Lord could do without our
intercession and our praise.
Yet it is the mystery of God that
He should require us,
His coworkers, to keep on praying
and never lose heart.

ROGER SCHUTZ

The Rule of Taizé

Our hands are so tiny
and the world's needs so vast
that we are forced back upon God,
who alone is sufficient.

Arthur Gossip

In the Secret Place of the Most High

A Christian fellowship lives and exists
by the intercession of its members
for one another, or it collapses.
I can no longer condemn
or hate a brother for whom I pray,
no matter how much trouble he causes me.

DIETRICH BONHOEFFER
Life Together

Real prayer is
life creating and life changing.

RICHARD FOSTER

The Disciplines of Prayer

The quality of a man's prayer is
determined by the state of his living.

WATCHMAN NEE

The Spiritual Man

Pray so that there is a real continuity
between your prayer and
your whole actual life.

P. T. FORSYTH
The Soul of Prayer

It is not so true that
"prayer changes things"
as that prayer changes me,
and I change things.

OSWALD CHAMBERS
My Utmost for His Highest

Prayer is not a method of using God;
rather is prayer a means of
reporting for duty to God.

CHARLES L. ALLEN
Prayer Changes Things

I see that prayerlessness is one
of my greatest sins of omission.
I am too short, ask too little,
ask too much want of forethought. . .
too little meditation upon Scripture.

ANDREW BONAR

The Diary and Life of Andrew Bonar

Don't take too much upon yourself
lest the spirit should get tired. . . .
It is sufficient to grasp one part from which
you can strike a spark in your heart.

MARTIN LUTHER

A Simple Way to Pray, for a Good Friend

Any method, absolutely any method, is your method
if you find it opens the doors toward heaven
and helps you gain contact with God.
And it is not your method,
no matter who does it,
if it does not succeed in doing that.

FRANK LAUBACH
Channels of Spiritual Power

Every time that is not seized upon
by some other duty is
seasonable enough for prayer.

JEREMY TAYLOR

Holy Living

Love to pray—
feel often during the day the need for prayer,
and take trouble to pray.
Prayer enlarges the heart until it is
capable of containing God's gift of Himself.

MOTHER TERESA

A Gift for God

And we must recognize that we are
heard not for our much speaking
but for our purity of heart.
Therefore our prayer must be brief and pure—
unless it chance be prolonged with
the inspiration of God's grace.

BENEDICT OF NURSIA

Rule of Saint Benedict

For to this day I drink of
the Lord's Prayer like a child—
drink and eat like an old man;
I can never get enough of it.
To me it is the best of all prayers,
even above the Psalms,
though I love them very much.

MARTIN LUTHER

A Simple Way to Pray, for a Good Friend

"Thy will be done on earth as it is in heaven."
When you say this in your pew on Sunday,
it means nothing unless you live it on Monday.

BILLY SUNDAY

The Lord's Prayer, in the King James Version,
contains only sixty-six words.
It can be repeated in less than a minute.
Despite its brevity,
it has been an enormous benefit to multitudes
of men and women.

W. PHILIP KELLER

A Layman Looks at the Lord's Prayer

. . .nothing is so costly, so exorbitant, so extortionate,
as that which is bought by prayer.
While, on the other hand,
nothing is so truly and everlastingly enriching
as that which is gotten and held by prayer,
and by prayer alone.

ALEXANDER WHYTE
Lord, Teach Us to Pray

God's best gifts, like valuable jewels,

are kept under lock and key,

and those who want them must,

with fervent faith, importunately ask for them;

for God is a rewarder of them

that diligently seek Him.

D. L. MOODY

Moody's Stories, Volume 2

A prayer to be said when
the world has gotten you down
and you feel rotten,
and you're too doggone tired to pray,
and you're in a big hurry, and besides,
you're mad at everybody: help.

CHARLES SWINDOLL

Growing Strong in the Seasons of Life

Many a man will make
promises to God in his extremity
but forget them in his prosperity.

BILLY SUNDAY

Prayer is to be studied—
If I had an invitation to visit the queen and was told
I might ask what I pleased of Her Majesty,
I should prepare my request. . . .
When you go before God,
it is well to know what you want.

CHARLES H. SPURGEON

Barbed Arrows

When you get whacked with a problem,
open yourself to a deeper relationship to the Lord.
Don't focus on the problem
but on the Lord's presence and power.

LLOYD OGILVIE

Let God Love You

If you are a stranger to prayer,
you are a stranger to the greatest source
of power known to human beings.

Someone has said that when we work, we work,
but when we pray, God works.

BILL HYBELS

Too Busy Not to Pray

No one can believe how powerful prayer is
and what it is able to effect except those who
have learned it by experience.

Table Talk

Prayer is spiritual dynamite.

HELEN SMITH SHOEMAKER
The Secret of Effective Prayer

A prayerless Christian is
a powerless Christian.

BILLY GRAHAM

Peace with God

The psalmists, in telling everyone
to praise God, are doing what all men do
when they speak of what they care about.

C. S. LEWIS

Reflections on the Psalms

It is therefore easy to understand why
the Book of Psalms is the favorite book of all the
saints. For every man on every occasion
can find in it Psalms which fit his needs,
which he feels to be as appropriate as if
they had been set there just for his sake.

MARTIN LUTHER
Preface to the Psalms

One of the values in becoming familiar with
the Psalms is that they gradually
become our own prayers.
When we meditate on the Psalms
with some regularity, we find that they
express our own feelings.

WILLIAM O. PAULSELL
Taste and See

The Psalms are the school for people learning to pray.
Fundamentally, prayer is our response
to God who speaks to us.
God's Word is always first.
He gets the first word in, always.
We answer.

EUGENE PETERSON

Under the Unpredictable Plant

Let us recollect for whom and for what
we prayed in secret this morning—
or did not pray.
Let us recall what we read,
what we heard, and with what feelings—
with Whom we conversed, and about what. . . .

ALEXANDER WHYTE

Lord, Teach Us to Pray

In my experience,

the practice of written meditation can be of great help

in bridging the gap between our two worlds,

the spiritual and the material. . . .

Writing something down also makes it more real.

If I do not write,

my meditation is likely to

remain vague and nebulous.

PAUL TOURNIER

The Adventure of Living

Self-centered prayers become manifestly self-centered,
even to us, when seen on paper.
Insights that are hazy figures on the horizon
sometimes become crystal clear when
committed to a journal.

RICHARD FOSTER
Freedom of Simplicity

If you are willing to commit your prayer to paper,
you probably really mean it. . . .
To write it down is one step in self-committal.

E. STANLEY JONES
Abundant Living

I suggest that we try listening to God
on the border lines of sleep. . . .
Many writers have a pen and paper ready
at their bedsides to record their inspirations
before their treacherous memories lose
what comes to them.

FRANK LAUBACH

Channels of Spiritual Power

The Lord let in much light.
Many sweet truths I wrote down.

THOMAS SHEPARD
Meditations

If the Holy Spirit should come when these thoughts
are in your mind and begin to preach to your heart,
giving you rich and enlightened thoughts,
then give Him His honor.
Let your preconceived ideas go;
be quiet and listen to Him who can talk better
than you, and note what He proclaims
and write it down, so will you experience miracles.

MARTIN LUTHER

A Simple Way to Pray, for a Good Friend

I proceeded further in reading my
old private writings and found that they had
the same effect upon me as before.
I could not but rejoice and bless God
for what passed long ago,
which, without writing, had been entirely lost.

DAVID BRAINERD

Memoirs

At the end of each month
I read over my prayer journal and see
where God had done miraculous things. . . .
If I can list a number of answers to
specific prayers in January,
I feel better prepared to trust God in February.

BILL HYBELS

Too Busy Not to Pray

To be "silent unto God" does not mean
drifting into mere feeling or sinking into reverse,
but deliberately getting into the center of things
and focusing on God.

Oswald Chambers
The Place of Help

The stilled voice learns to hold to peace;
to listen with the heart to silence, that is joy.

MADELEINE L'ENGLE
The Weather of the Heart

Inward silence renders
possible our conversation with Jesus Christ.

ROGER SCHUTZ
The Rule of Taizé

Get alone with God.

Seek some secluded spot.

Close the inner door to the inner room

of your inner spirit.

Be still. Be silent. Be serene.

W. PHILIP KELLER

Walking with God

Before there can be meaningful conversation with
God, we must take time to wait on the Lord
in silent expectation.

DONALD G. BLOESCH

The Struggle of Prayer

We need the channel of silence to transport us
from the busy harbors of our own tensions
out to the ocean of God's infinite being.

MARVA J. DAWN

Reaching Out without Dumbing Down

In silence and quiet, the devout soul profiteth
and learneth the secrets of the Scriptures.

THOMAS À KEMPIS

The Imitation of Christ

Two friends can be together in the silence
with genuine creativity in solace or joy or supplication.
In my heart, I ask Him to do this or that.
He also asks me.

EUGENIA PRICE

Another Day

God's methods don't change because
we are so noisy and busy.
He is longing for your attention,
your individual and full attention. . . .
He will wait and wait until
you finally sit in silence and listen.

CHARLES SWINDOLL

Growing Strong in the Seasons of Life

We are silent at the beginning of the day
because God should have the first word,
and we are silent before going to sleep
because the last word also belongs to God.

DIETRICH BONHOEFFER

Life Together

Prayer is not a means by which
I seek to control God;
it is a means of putting myself in
a position where God can control me.

CHARLES L. ALLEN
Prayer Changes Things

I will renounce my will, my inclinations,
my whims and fancies
and make myself a willing slave
to the will of God.

MOTHER TERESA

A Gift for God

I would a thousand times rather that
God's will should be done than my own.
I cannot see into the future as God can;
therefore, it is a good deal better to let Him
choose for me than to choose for myself.

D. L. MOODY

Prevailing Prayer

The people of true prayer are
those who can see the answer when
it is given in God's way,
not theirs.

HELEN SMITH SHOEMAKER
The Secret of Effective Prayer

God will be responsible for our feelings
if we will hand them over to Him.

CATHERINE MARSHALL
Something More

Prayer, at long last, is an altar and an oblation. . . .
By this surrender prayer finds a
"service which is perfect freedom."
In this loss, prayer wins its richest gain.

GEORGE A. BUTTRICK
Prayer

When we omit thanksgiving from our prayers,
we rob God of an honor due Him,
and we render our prayers powerless.

LEHMAN STRAUSS

Sense and Nonsense about Prayer

We are surrounded by God's benefits.
The best use of these benefits is
our unceasing expression of gratitude.

JOHN CALVIN

Institutes of the Christian Religion

In our daily practice of prayer,
we should begin each day with
an act of loving thankfulness to God.

C. F. ANDREWS

Christ and Prayer

When I go to God, I want to thank Him,
first and most,
for the kindness that remembers me
even when I forget Him.

ARTHUR GOSSIP

In the Secret Place of the Most High

I have learned a great deal about prayer,
praying for other people when the need arises,
spontaneously and immediately. . . .
We can share with each other without
being threatened by each other's differences
because we know that we are united by Christ,
and this union is a union of love and not fear.

MADELEINE L'ENGLE
The Rock that Is Higher

It is in the union and fellowship of believers
that the Spirit can manifest His full power.

ANDREW MURRAY

With Christ in the School of Prayer

God likes to see His people shut up to this,
that there is no hope but in prayer.
Herein lies the Church's power against the world.

ANDREW BONAR

The Diary and Life of Andrew Bonar

The devil smiles when we make plans.
He laughs when we get too busy.
But he trembles when we pray—
especially when we pray together.